Aldus PageMa
Training Guide

Wendy Chuter

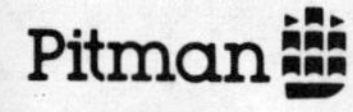

PITMAN PUBLISHING
128 Long Acre, London, WC2E 9AN

A Division of Longman Group UK Limited

First published in Great Britain 1991

British Library Cataloguing in Publication Data
Chuter, Wendy
Aldus PageMaker: Training guide.
I. Title
070.50285

ISBN 0 273 03423 5

Typeset by TA Tek Art Ltd, Addiscombe, Croydon, Surrey
Printed and bound in Great Britain

Contents

Introduction

Aldus PageMaker is a desk top publishing software program which enables the user to produce professional looking hard copy ready for reproduction.

Text can be entered into a word processing program and then placed into the publication, or entered directly into PageMaker. A variety of fonts and pitch sizes can be used and simple graphics, such as lines, boxes, circles and shading can be drawn easily. There are facilities for scanned graphical images, such as pictures and diagrams, to be imported into the publication. Once an image has been placed, its size and position can be altered. Text can be arranged into a designated number of columns and there are a variety of ways of wrapping text around graphics.

In this guide

PageMaker uses a mouse and pull down menus but these menus can also be accessed by using the keyboard. This *Training Guide* will only give instructions for the use of the mouse. When the keyboard or the mouse buttons need to be pressed the command will be shown in CAPS throughout the guide. The necessary Menu options will be shown in bold.

Getting started

It is assumed that you have installed PageMaker and Windows on your hard disk in sub-directories **C: \ PM** and **C: \ WINDOWS** respectively. From DOS access the **Windows** sub-directory and enter WIN PM and then press ENTER.

Using the mouse

The mouse is the small input device, used sometimes in conjunction with the keyboard, to perform many of PageMaker's actions. As you move the mouse across your work surface a pointer moves on your screen in the same direction. Lifting the mouse does not move the pointer. If the mouse bumps against something or you have insufficient room on the work surface, lift the mouse, put it down where there is more room and continue working.

The mouse can have two or three buttons. All PageMaker actions require the use of only one button at a time. The left button is the main mouse button, whether the mouse has two or three buttons. The right button is used to toggle between **Fit in window** and **Actual size** displays on the screen. The mouse can be used for almost everything, except typing text and numbers. There are four mouse button techniques and these will be referred to in this way throughout this Training Guide.

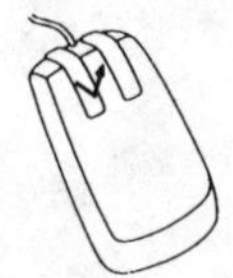

CLICK Press the mouse button once

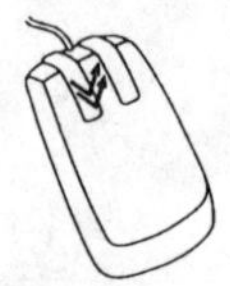

DOUBLE CLICK Press the mouse button twice in quick succession

PRESS Hold the button down

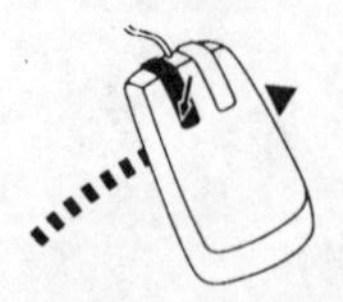

DRAG Hold the button down and drag the mouse across the work surface

The Menus

When you position the pointer at any point in the menu title and CLICK, a menu will drop down. You will then see the list of options connected with the particular menu. To select from the pulled down menu, POINT and CLICK the left mouse button at the required option. If you change your mind after selecting a menu, either select a different menu or CLICK anywhere away from the pulled down menu.

Note If any of the menu options are selected before you request a new publication or open an existing publication, the default settings will be altered.

Screen display

Unless you choose the **Fit in window** display you will only see part of your publication on the screen at a time. To change the type of display on the screen, POINT and CLICK the left button at the **Page menu**. You will then have a choice of five sizes of display. You may need to scroll your page on the screen in order to see another part. This can be done by:

- CLICKING on the scroll arrows in the desired direction
- DRAGGING the white box in the scroll bars
- CLICKING in the grey area of the scroll bars to jump a fixed amount.

If the right mouse button is pressed at any time it will change the view from **any** size to **Actual** size. If pressed again in **Actual** size the view will change to **Fit in window** size.

Task 1 **Creating a new publication**

Objective To set up the page specifications.

Instructions Before you can start keying text into a new publication the page needs to be set up. You need to stipulate the size and orientation of the paper you wish to print out on, the margins, the number of pages required in the publication and whether you want double-sided or facing pages. The settings can be changed at any time by selecting the **Page setup** option from the **File menu**.

Activity 1.1 You are going to set up a single page, A4 portrait publication with equal margins on all sides.

1 CLICK on **File** in the menu bar to pull down this menu.

2 CLICK on **New** to select a new publication. A display similar to the following should appear.

Page setup [O K]

Page size: ○ Letter ○ Legal ○ Tabloid [Cancel]

◉ A4 ○ A3 ○ A5 ○ B5

Custom:

Orientation: Tall Wide

Start page #: [1] **# of pages:** [1]

Options: ☐ Double-sided ☐ Facing pages

Margin in mm: Inside [25] Outside [25]

Top [25] Bottom [25]

Target printer: PostScript Printer on COM1:

Instructions

The following options are available at the **Page setup menu**. You will be selecting only some of these options at the moment. An explanation of these follows.

Page size: this enables you to select from seven predefined page sizes or customise your own.

Orientation: this enables you to select whether the paper should be taller than it is wide (portrait), or wider than it is tall (landscape).

Start page: this enables the setting of the value for automatic page numbering and the number of pages required in the publication.

Option: the double-sided option enables you to create a publication which will be reproduced on both sides of the paper. The inside margin alternates from being on the left for right-hand pages to the right on left pages.

Facing pages: this allows the viewing of pages which will face each other in the publication.

Margin: this enables the setting of the margins for all your pages in the publication.

Activity 1.2

Enter the following settings for your publication. A filled-in circle, or a cross in the box denotes that it has been selected.

1 If the circle by the **A4** setting does not have a filled-in circle, POINT and CLICK at it to select it.

2 If the circle by the **Tall** orientation does not have a filled-in circle, POINT and CLICK at it to select it.

3 The boxes for the **Start page** and **Number of pages** should show **1** in each box. If they do not, POINT and CLICK in each box. If necessary press DELETE to delete the other figure and enter the figure **1**.

4 If the double-sided setting has a cross in its box, POINT and CLICK at the box to remove it.

5 The margins need to be set at 25 mm all round. If these are not the current settings, POINT and CLICK in each box, and if necessary DELETE the other figure(s) and enter **25**.

6 CLICK on **OK**.

A display similar to the following should appear.

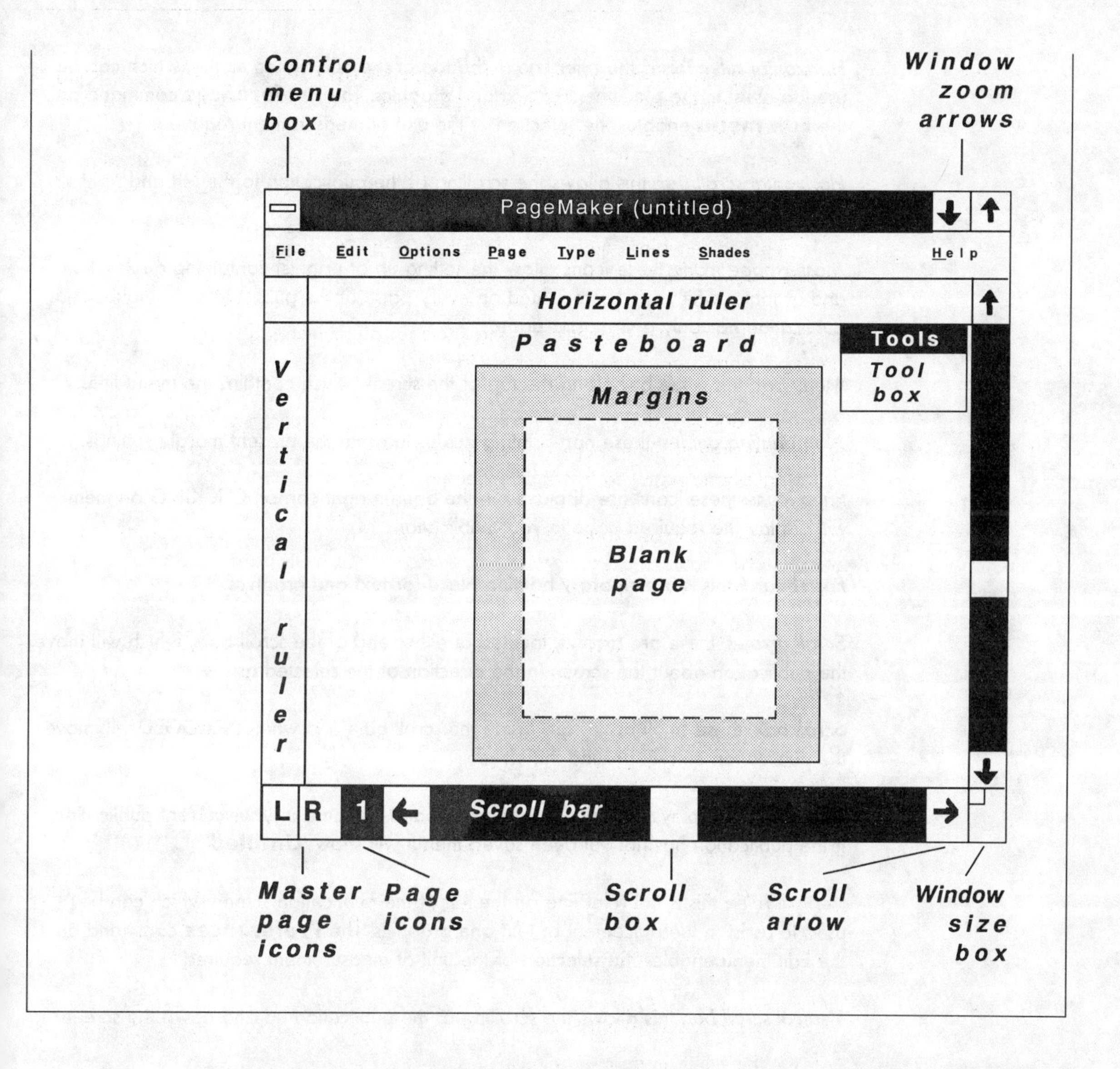

Instructions

The following section explains the layout of the screen and the terms which will be used in this *Training Guide*.

Blank page: this is an empty page displayed at **Fit in window size**.

Control menu box: this is the small square displayed in the top left corner which enables you to use the **Windows** software and is another way of exiting from PageMaker.

Dotted lines in the rulers: this indicates the exact position of the pointer on the page. The pointer is moved by using the mouse.

Floating toolbox palette: this contains the icons for the tools needed when you work with text and graphics. It can be moved to another position on the screen by DRAGGING the title bar (Tools) to the required position.

Horizontal ruler: this is the ruler line at the top of the publication screen which can be used to assist in the placement of text and graphics. The **Preferences** command on the **Edit menu** enables the selection of the unit of measurement required.

Horizontal scroll bar: this allows the scrolling of the publication to the left and right of the screen.

Master page icons: these icons allow the setting up of page(s) containing guides, text and graphics which will be repeated on every page of the publication. A single-sided publication has only one master page.

Menu bar: this is the bar along the top of the screen which contains the menu titles.

Non-printing guides: these non-printing guides indicate the present margin settings.

Page icons: these icons are displayed in the bottom right corner, CLICKING on them will display the required page in your publication.

Pasteboard: this is a temporary holding-place for text and graphics.

Scroll arrows: these are arrows, located at either end of the scroll bars, which will move the publication about the screen in the direction of the selected arrow.

Scroll box: these small boxes are inside the scroll bars and when DRAGGED will move the publication quickly around the screen.

Title bar: this displays the drive, sub-directory and filename of your current publication. If the publication has not yet been saved then it will show '**Untitled**'.

Vertical ruler: this is the ruler line on the left of the publication screen which can be used to assist in the placement of text and graphics. The **Preferences** command on the Edit menu enables the selection of the unit of measurement required.

Vertical scroll bar: this allows the scrolling of the publication up and down the screen.

Window box size: this box enables the adjustment of the size of the PageMaker window by dragging on the box.

Window zoom arrows: these enable you to minimise (down arrow) PageMaker to an icon, or to maximise (up arrow) the PageMaker icon into a full window.

Zero point: this enables the repositioning of the zero point which helps with measurements and remembering locations.

Zero point marker: this displays the intersection of the vertical and horizontal rulers.

Activity 1.3

Your publication page should now be displayed on the screen at **Fit in window** size. It is difficult to read text in this display; 75% is much easier, so change the size of the screen display. When you have changed the display it may be necessary to scroll the publication on the screen so that you can see the top of your publication page ready for use.

1 CLICK on **Page** in the menu bar.

2 CLICK on **75% size.**

3 CLICK on the **horizontal arrow** at the end of the horizontal scroll bar until you can see both left and right margins.

4 CLICK on the up pointing arrow ↑ at the top of the vertical scroll bar, under the word **Help**, until you can see the top margin.

Key words

New
Screen view size
Scrolling

Task 2 **Entering text and saving the publication**

Objective

To enter text into the publication, correct any errors and save the publication for future use.

Instructions

You are going to type a menu and then save it. This menu will then be recalled and used in future tasks. Type the text first, ignoring any typing errors and press ENTER to start a new line when required. This will keep your text as one block. If you position and click the text pointer on each new line it will be seen as a separate block with its own handles. You are going to change the text appearance and alignment in later tasks.

Activity 2.1

1 CLICK on the **text tool** in the toolbox.

2 POINT and CLICK the text pointer on to the page just below your top margin.

3 Key in the following text, keeping the line spacing the same and ignoring any keying in errors.

MENU

August 19–

*****

Tomato Soup
Melon
Pate
Prawn Cocktail

*****

Roast Spring Chicken
Fried Fillet of Plaice
Rump Steak
Vegetarian Quiche

*****

Selection of Fresh Vegetables
Creamed or French Fried Potatoes

*****

Fresh Fruit Salad
Cheesecake
Black Forest Gateau

*****

£8.95 per person

Identify any errors you have made and correct them in the following way:

If it is the last character typed press BACKSPACE.

If you wish to delete a character in the middle of a word, position and CLICK the text pointer to the *right* of the incorrect character, and press BACKSPACE.

If you wish to insert a character, position and CLICK the text pointer to the right of the missing character, then type the missing letter.

If you wish to insert a line space, position and CLICK the text pointer at the beginning of the line you wish to move down and press ENTER.

If you wish to delete a line space, position and CLICK the text pointer at the beginning of the line you wish to move up and press BACKSPACE.

Activity 2.3 Now save your publication for future use.

1 CLICK on **File**.

2 CLICK on **Save**.

A display similar to the following should appear.

```
Save publication as                          [ O K ]
_______________________________
                                             [ Cancel ]

        Directories:
        [..]
        [PIF]            Path: C:\WINDOWS
        [-A-]
        [-B-]            Name: [          ]
        [-C-]
             Save as: (•) Publication  ( ) Template
```

Instructions The following options are available at the **Save menu** and are explained as follows.

Directories: this enables the selection of the **drive** and **sub-directory** in which the publication will be saved.

Path: this denotes the **current drive** and **sub-directory** in which the publication will be saved.

Name: this allows the **name** of the publication to be inserted using up to eight characters.

Publication: this **saves** the collection of pages containing **text** and **graphics** for future use.

Template: this **saves** the publication **as a template** with the extension PT3. When this file is opened in future it will appear untitled on the screen, so that you can save it under another filename and leave the template unchanged for future use.

When using the **Save** option the old version on the disk will automatically be saved with the new version currently held in the computer's memory.

If using the **Save as** option you will be allowed to save the publication under a different filename.

1 CLICK in the **name box** and key in **MENU** as the filename.

2 CLICK on **publication** if it is not already selected.

3 CLICK on **OK**.

Activity 2.4 When you wish to stop working on a publication it should be closed. However, selecting either the **open** or **exit** options has the same effect.

1 CLICK on **File**.

2 CLICK on **Close**.

Key words

Entering text
Correcting typing errors
Save
Close

Task 3

Opening a publication and changing the type specifications

Objective

To open a publication and change existing text into a different font and type size.

Instructions

You are going to open the publication containing the menu from the previous task and change the appearance of the text to make the display more effective.

Activity 3.1

1 CLICK on **File**.

2 CLICK on **Open**.

A display similar to the following should appear.

Open publication

O K

Cancel

Files/Directories:

CHUTER.PM3
MENU.PM3
WENDY.PM3
[..]
[PM]

Path: C:\WINDOWS

Name:

Open: ⊙ Original ○ Copy

Instructions

The following options are available at the **Open menu**:

Original: this enables you to work with the **last saved version** of the file.

Copy: this enables you to work on a copy of the publication which will then appear as untitled on the screen.

Activity 3.2 You are going to work on your original publication. If necessary, CLICK on the scroll arrows until the filename **MENU** is displayed.

1 **DOUBLE** CLICK on **MENU**.

2 Display the publication at 75% page size.

3 Scroll the publication by CLICKING on the required arrow(s) until both left and right margins can be seen.

4 Scroll the publication, by CLICKING on the required arrow, until the top of the publication can be seen.

Instructions You are going to change the word **MENU** at the top of your publication to a larger type size and a different font. The date should be underlined and the price printed in italics. It is not necessary to key in text before changing its style and font; the options can be selected first and text entered afterwards.

To change text you need to select it first. It will then appear in 'reverse video' (i.e. white lettering on a black background) on the screen. Below are a number of ways of selecting text using the text tool. You will need to select the three pieces of text separately as they do not run on from each other.

Activity 3.3 To select a **range of text** *character-by-character* or *line-by-line*, position the text pointer at the beginning of the range and DRAG the text pointer.

To select a **required word**, position the text pointer on the word and DOUBLE CLICK.

To select a **required paragraph**, position the text pointer anywhere within the paragraph and TRIPLE CLICK.

To select a **range of text**, position the text pointer at the beginning of the range, CLICK, hold down SHIFT and CLICK again at the end of the range.

To select all the text **within a block of handles**, CLICK the text pointer anywhere within the text, CLICK on **Edit menu** and then CLICK on **Select all**.

To **cancel** a selection, either select something else, or CLICK on a **blank** area of the page or the **pasteboard**, otherwise select a different tool from the toolbox.

1 CLICK on the text tool.

2 DOUBLE CLICK on the word **MENU**.

3 CLICK on **Type**.

4 CLICK on **Type specs**.

A display similar to the following should appear.

```
Type specifications                              (O K)

                                                 (Cancel)
Font name and size:

 Courier        8
 Elite          9              Size:
 Helv          10              [12]   points
 Pica          12              Leading:
 Tms Rmn       14              [Auto] points

                                  [ ] Auto leading

Type style:               Position:          Case:

[X] Normal  [ ] Underline   (•) Normal       (•) Normal
[ ] Bold    [ ] Strikethru  ( ) Superscript  ( ) All caps
[ ] Italic  [ ] Reverse     ( ) Subscript    ( ) Small caps
```

The current font and size will appear in reverse video (white text on a black background). The **present type style** will have a cross in its box and the **present position** and **case** will have a filled-in circle. You may need to click on the relevant scroll arrows to display the different fonts and sizes.

5 CLICK on **Helv** or any other font you may have displayed.

6 CLICK on **18** or the nearest size available.

7 CLICK on **Bold** in the **Type style**.

8 CLICK on **OK**.

Your word **MENU** will remain highlighted.

9 TREBLE CLICK on the **date line**.

10 CLICK on **Type**.

11 CLICK on **Underline**.

12 Scroll down the publication and TREBLE CLICK on the **price line**.

13 CLICK on **Type**.

14 CLICK on **italics**.

15 **Save** your publication for future use and call it **MENU**.

Key words	**Open**
	Selecting text with the text tool
	Type specifications

Task 4 Changing the horizontal alignment of text

Objective

To change the horizontal alignment of text between the left and right margins.

Instructions

You are going to change the positioning of the lines. When you begin keying in the text it is normally aligned to the left margin. You are going to centre all your text horizontally with just the date aligned to the left and the price aligned to the right. You can, if you wish, set the alignment before keying in the text.

Activity 4.1

Change all the alignment of the present text to the centre. It will be easier to do this while in '**Fit in window**' size.

1 Open your publication called **MENU**.

2 DOUBLE CLICK on the **right button** to display at **Fit in window** size.

3 Select the **text tool** from the toolbox and CLICK the text pointer anywhere in the text.

4 CLICK on **Edit**.

5 CLICK on **Select all** to select all of the text within the block.

6 CLICK on **Type**.

7 CLICK on **Align centre**.

Activity 4.2

Now change the alignment of the date to the left and the price to the right to enhance the layout. You may find it easier to change the screen display to a larger size.

1 Position the **text pointer** on the **date**.

2 TREBLE CLICK to highlight the **date**.

3 CLICK on **Type**.

4 CLICK on **Align left**.

5 Position the **text pointer** on the **price**.

6 TREBLE CLICK to highlight the **price per head**.

7 CLICK on **Type**.

8 CLICK on **Align right**.

9 **Save** your publication for future use, calling it **MENU**.

Key words **Align centre**
Align left
Align right

Task 5 Using ruler guides

Objective

To use ruler guides to assist in positioning an object on the page and to lock the ruler guides into position.

Instructions

You are going to use guidelines to help you move text in the next task. The menu will look better if you centre it vertically on the page. Also, in a later exercise you are going to reduce the width of a block of text in order to draw a decorative box around the menu. However, you could, if you wish, just position the text 'by eye'. The guidelines will only appear on the screen, not on the printed copy, and up to 40 guidelines can be used in a publication. The vertical guidelines will be used to help reduce the width of the block of text. Guidelines are obtained by POINTING at the relevant ruler and DRAGGING them to the required position. Any guidelines set will be saved with the publication. If you wish to remove them at any time, select the **pointer tool**, POINT at them and DRAG them back to their relevant rulers.

Activity 5.1

You are going to set two horizontal and two vertical guidelines to help you later. The horizontal guidelines will help to centre the text vertically on the page. The vertical guidelines will help when altering the width of the text block.

1 Open your publication called **MENU**.

2 CLICK on the **pointer tool**.

3 POINT at the **horizontal ruler**, DRAG a **guideline** down to **60 mm** on the vertical ruler.

4 POINT at the **horizontal ruler**, DRAG another **guideline** down to **240 mm** on the vertical ruler.

5 POINT at the **vertical ruler** and DRAG a **guideline** across to **35 mm** on the horizontal ruler.

6 POINT at the **vertical ruler** and DRAG another guideline across to **175 mm** on the horizontal ruler.

Instructions

These guidelines can be moved very easily by POINTING the **pointer tool** at them and DRAGGING them to a new position. If you do this accidentally, use the **Undo** command on the **Edit menu**. However, this problem can be prevented by locking the guides into position. If you wish to remove or move the guidelines after they have been locked, then **deselect** the **Lock guides** on the **Options menu**. This will remove the tick, and then the guidelines can be DRAGGED back to their respective rulers. The guidelines can also be set to have a 'snap to' effect. These guides then exert a magnetic pull on an object.

Activity 5.2

1 CLICK on **Options**.

2 CLICK on **Lock guides** (if a tick appears alongside it means the option is already selected).

3 CLICK on **Options**.

4 CLICK on **Snap to guides** (if a tick appears alongside it means the option is already selected).

5 **Save** your publication for future use, calling it **MENU**.

Key words

Ruler guides
Lock guides
Snap to guides

Task 6 Moving a text block

Objectives To use the pointer tool to move a text block.

Instructions You are going to move your text block down the page to the guidelines you set in the previous task. To move the block select it first by putting handles on it. By pointing at your text and keeping the left mouse button depressed a four-headed arrow icon will appear. This will enable the objects to be moved about the page. These handles will look as follows:

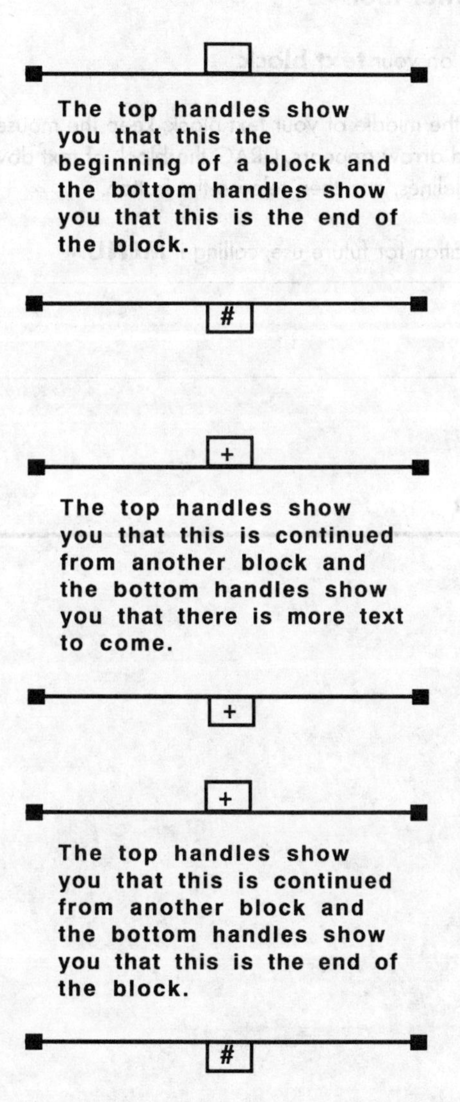

The four black rectangles at the end of the lines are called **handles**.
The horizontal lines with loops are called **windowshades**.
An empty loop indicates it is the beginning of the block of text.

The following is an explanation of the different types of handles and windowshades possible.

A + in the **top loop** indicates that the text is continued from another block.
A + in the **bottom loop** indicates that there is more text to come in another block.
A # in the **bottom loop** indicates the end of the text in that block.
To **deselect** a block either CLICK on another block, or select a **different tool**, otherwise CLICK on the **pasteboard**.

Activity

1 CLICK on the **pointer tool**.

2 POINT and CLICK on your **text block**.

3 POINT roughly in the middle of your text block, keep the mouse button depressed until a four-headed arrow appears, DRAG the block of text down until it snaps to the horizontal guidelines, and then release the button.

4 **Save** your publication for future use, calling it **MENU**.

Key words

Text block
Handles
Windowshades
Moving an object

Task 7 Altering a text block width

Objective

To change the width of a text block.

Instructions

If you draw a decorative box around your non-printing margin guides, your date and price will be touching the edge of the box. You therefore need to make the current width of your block of text smaller so this does not happen. This is done by POINTING at one of the **handles** and keeping the mouse button depressed until a two-headed arrow appears. This icon enables you to DRAG the handles on the text inwards to make the line length smaller. Make sure you do not make the length of the block smaller or it will look as though you have lost the bottom of the text. If this happens, put handles on the text and DRAG the + in the bottom windowshade down to restore it to its original length. The vertical guidelines set previously will assist you with this.

Activity

1 Open the publication called **MENU**.

2 Change the window display to **Fit in window**.

3 CLICK on the **pointer tool**.

4 POINT and CLICK at your **text block** to put handles on it.

5 POINT at one of the **left handles** and keep the left mouse button depressed until a two-headed arrow appears, then DRAG until you reach the vertical guideline. Take care not to reduce the length of the text block.

6 POINT at one of the **right handles** and keep the left mouse button depressed until a two-headed arrow appears, then DRAG until you reach the vertical guideline. Take care not to reduce the length of the text block.

7 **Save** your publication for future use, calling it **MENU**.

Key words **Altering block width**

Task 8 **Drawing boxes**

Objective

To draw a box with square corners, amend the choice of line style and change to rounded corners.

Instructions

You are going to improve the appearance of the publication by drawing a square box around the menu and selecting the style of line you require. The different available styles of lines are displayed when the **Line menu** is selected. You will also see that once drawn, the corners and the style of line can be changed. The box is drawn by selecting the relevant tool from the toolbox, positioning the pointer at one of the corners to start drawing from and DRAGGING until you reach the required size. If you release the button too soon the size of the box will be formed before you are ready. The box can be deleted by putting handles on it and pressing DELETE. Alternatively, the size of the box can be adjusted by putting handles on it, and DRAGGING at the handles until the required size is achieved.

Activity 8.1

1 Open your publication called **MENU**.

2 Change the screen display to **Fit in window** so that it is easier to see the size of box required.

3 CLICK on the **square box tool** in the toolbox.

4 CLICK on **Lines**.

5 CLICK on **4 pt** for the thickness of the line.

6 Position the **box pointer** at the top left corner of your margin guides and DRAG across the publication until you reach the bottom right corner. Take care not to release the button until you have reached the required position.

Activity 8.2

Now you are going to change your box to have a different style of line and rounded corners. Before you can change these you need to put handles on the box to select it. If you do not have handles on the box at present, select the **pointer tool** and point and CLICK at your box. While you have handles on it you can also change the style of line.

1 CLICK on **Lines**.

2 CLICK on the **double line**.

3 CLICK on **Options**.

4 CLICK on **Rounded corners**.

5 Select one of the styles of rounded corners by POINTING and CLICKING on it.

6 CLICK on **OK**.

7 **Save** the publication for future use, calling it **MENU**.

Key words	**Square corner boxes** **Rounded corner boxes** **Line styles**

Task 9

Printing your publication

Objective

To obtain a hard copy of your publication.

Instructions

You have produced a menu which you would like to print out. It is always good practice to save the publication before printing in case there are any difficulties. This will prevent the loss of your work.

Activity

1 Open the publication called **MENU**.

2 CLICK on **File**.

3 CLICK on **Print**. A display similar to the following should appear.

Print

O K

Copies: 1 Collate Reverse order

Cancel

Setup

Pages: ◉ All From 1 to 1

Scaling: percent

Options: ☐ Thumbnails ☐ Bit-map smoothing ☐ Fast rules

☐ Crop marks ☐ Spot color overlays ☐ Cutouts

☐ Tile ○ Manual ○ Auto overlap ☐ mm

Printer: Epson FX-80 on LPT1:
Hewlett Packard

Paper size:
368.3 x 296.7

Orientation:
Landscape

The main options available on the **Print menu** are now explained.

Copies: this enables the **number of copies** of each page to be specified.

Collate: this enables the printing of **one complete copy** of the publication before printing the next one. This is useful when you want to review the first copy while the other copies are printing, and saves time sorting the copies manually.

Reverse order: this enables the **printing out** of the publication **in reverse order** so that the pages are in the correct sequence.

Pages All: this enables all the pages in the publication to be printed.

Pages From: this enables only a part of your publication to be specified by entering the start and finish page numbers.

Printer: this is the list of printers that can be used to print out. The highlighted printer is the one selected at the moment.

Orientation: this indicates the orientation of the paper on which you are going to print and should match the requirements of the publication. If they do not match you will need to CLICK on the **Setup box**, select the necessary alterations and CLICK on **OK**.

4 CHECK that you have requested: one copy, all pages. Ensure the orientation is portrait.

5 CLICK on **OK**.

Key words	**Print**

Task 10 Using the *Write* word processing program within the Windows software

Objective

To use the *Microsoft Windows* program to produce word processed text which will be used in a future task.

Instructions

If you wish, you can key in text while in *PageMaker*. Alternatively, you may find it quicker to use a word processor which has the facility to spell check. If you find that various codes appear in the text when you import it, you may need to save your word processed file as an **ASCII** file. Leave such items as bold and underline until you have imported your text into the publication.

Activity 10.1

You are going to reduce the *PageMaker* window to an icon and use the *Write* program to key in the text. By reducing the publication to an icon you will be able to move between the two programs without having to exit each time. When you reduce *PageMaker* to an icon you will have two icons displayed at the bottom of the screen: a disk and the *PageMaker* icon. To work with one of the programs, DOUBLE CLICK on the relevant icon.

1 To reduce the *PageMaker* window CLICK on the **horizontal bar** in the top left corner above the **File option**.

2 CLICK on **Minimise**.

3 DOUBLE CLICK on the **disk icon** to access the **Windows** program.

4 DOUBLE CLICK on the filename **WRITE.EXE** to access the word processing program called *Write*.

Activity 10.2

You are now going to key in the following text which will be used in a future task. You will then save the word processed text ready to place it into the *PageMaker* publication.

1 Key in the following text and correct any errors that you make.

THE CENTRAL PROCESSING UNIT

Otherwise known as the CPU. This is where all the work is done. It is, if you like, the 'brain' of the computer. It consists of four sections – a memory unit, an arithmetic logic unit, a control unit and clock.

DISK DRIVES

There are two main types of disk storage – floppy disk and hard disk. Drives for floppy disks use either:

disks of flexible plastic coated with magnetic material and enclosed in a cardboard sleeve or disks of flexible plastic coated with magnetic material and enclosed in a rigid plastic case.

The hard disk drives are totally sealed from the environment and it is not usual for the disks themselves to be removed from the CPU.

THE KEYBOARD

The most widely used form of input is the QWERTY keyboard. It is a means of communication between the operator and the computer.

THE MONITOR

Otherwise known as the Visual Display Unit (VDU). It is an output device which enables you to display results and messages on the screen rather than have them printed on to paper. VDUs vary in size, shape and colour according to the design of the manufacturer. The most common size displays 80 characters across and 24 lines down.

THE PRINTER

It is an output device which enables you to obtain a hard copy of your work. Printers can be separated into two main categories:

Impact printer – these work by applying pressure against a ribbon onto the paper and the contact made transfers ink from the ribbon to the paper to form the required image. Non-impact printer – these produce images without any physical impact being made on the paper.

2 CLICK on **File**.

3 CLICK on **Save**.

4 Key in **COMPUTER** as the filename in the relevant box.

5 CLICK on **OK**.

Activity 10.3

Now minimise the *Write* window and return to the *PageMaker* publication. When you minimise this time you may have two icons displayed: a **pencil** indicating the *Write* window and a **pasteboard** indicating the *PageMaker* window.

1 CLICK on the **horizontal bar** in the top left corner.

2 CLICK on **Minimise**.

3 DOUBLE CLICK on the ***PageMaker* icon** (the pasteboard) to open this window.

Key words ***Write*** **word processor**
Minimise windows

Task 11

Placing word processed text into a publication

Objective To import word processed text into a publication using the place facility.

Instructions You are going to place the text keyed in via the *Write* word processor. There are two main ways of placing text:

- *Manual flow:* when **autoflow** is *not* selected from the **Options menu** the placed text will flow to the bottom of the column or until it meets an object which blocks the text.
- *Autoflow:* when **autoflow** *is* selected from the **Options menu** the placed text will flow continuously until all the text is placed, creating new pages if necessary.

You will be using the Autoflow option in a later task.

Activity 11.1

1 CLICK on **File**.

2 CLICK on **New** and set up the following settings; **A4** page, **tall** size, *not* **double-sided**, *all margins* **25 mm**.

3 CLICK on **Options** and ensure that the **Autoflow** option is *not* selected. There should not be a tick alongside. If there is, CLICK on the option again to remove it.

4 CLICK on **File**.

5 CLICK on **Place**.

A display similar to the following should appear.

```
Place file                                  ( O K )
                                            ( Cancel )
Files/Directories:

CHUTER.PM3
MENU.PM3               Path: C:\WINDOWS
WENDY.PM3
[..]                   Name: [          ]
[PM]
                       Place:  (•) As new item

                               ( ) Replacing entire story

                               ( ) Inserting text

Options: [ ] Retain format [ ] Convert quotes  [ ] Read tags
```

Instructions

The following options are available at the **Place** menu. An explanation of these follows:

Retain format: this enables the format that you had in the word processor to be kept.

Convert quotes: this enables the 'straight' quotation marks to be converted into 'rounded' opening and closing quotation marks.

Read tags: this instructs *PageMaker* to read style tags that have been set up in the word processor.

Activity 11.2

1 DOUBLE CLICK on **COMPUTER.WRI**. If you cannot find this file the incorrect drive or sub-directory may be displayed.

2 CLICK the **manual text flow icon** at the top of the publication, making sure you are within the margins. The text should now be placed on the page.

3 **Save** the publication using the filename **COMPUTER** for future use.

Key words

Place
Autoflow

Task 12

Justifying text

Objective

To align text so that it is flush at both left and right margins.

Instructions

You are going to change the alignment of the text which has just been placed. If you look at it you will see that the text is straight at the left margin, but ragged at the right margin, provided it was not justified by the word processor. By highlighting the text it can be justified so that both sides will be flush with the margins. When text is highlighted you can, if you wish, change other items, such as the pitch and font.

Activity

1 CLICK on **File**.

2 Open the publication called **COMPUTER**.

3 Select the **text tool** from the toolbox.

4 CLICK the **text pointer** anywhere in the text.

5 CLICK on **Edit**.

6 CLICK on **Select all** to highlight all of the text in that block.

7 CLICK on **Type**.

8 CLICK on **Justify**.

The text should now be justified.

9 **Save** the file calling it **COMPUTER**.

Key words **Justify**

Task 13

Cutting and pasting text

Objective

To use the cut and paste technique to move text from one position to another.

Instructions

If you look at the text in the previous task you will see that the definitions of the computer terms are not in alphabetical order. You are going to use the cut and paste options to move the paragraphs concerning 'The Monitor' and 'The Printer' to the end of the text. When the cut option is used the selected object is put into the **Windows clipboard** ready for it to be pasted back into a different position. The clipboard is only a temporary storage area, therefore the present contents will be lost when another selected object is cut. This option can also be used to copy an object, the only difference being that the object remains in its original position and will be copied to another location. This option can also be used to cut or copy objects to other *PageMaker* publications.

Activity

1 CLICK on **File** and open the publication called **COMPUTER**.

2 Select the **text tool** from the toolbox.

3 CLICK the **text pointer** at the beginning of the text to be selected, i.e. **THE MONITOR**.

4 Move the **text pointer** to the end of the text to be selected, i.e. to the end of the paragraph concerning the printer.

5 Hold down SHIFT and CLICK to select the two paragraphs.

6 CLICK on **Edit**.

7 CLICK on **Cut**.

8 Position and CLICK the **text pointer** at the end of the paragraph concerning the keyboard.

9 Press ENTER twice to start a new paragraph.

10 CLICK on **Edit**.

11 CLICK on **Paste**.

You may need to look back through the text and insert or delete any necessary line spaces to tidy up the text.

12 **Save** the publication for future use, calling it **COMPUTER**.

Key words **Cut**
Paste

Task 14

Placing, sizing and moving a graphic

Objectives

To place a scanned graphic into text, adjust its size and change its position in the publication.

Instructions

Before starting this task you will need to scan the graphic depicting a computer, shown below. Name the scanned file **MODEL**. If you do not have access to a scanner you may find a graphic in the PMTUTOR sub-directory which you could use instead. You are going to place this scanned image into your previously saved publication called **COMPUTER**. When the graphic is placed the text will overlap it. In future tasks you will see that the text can be made to jump over or wrap around the graphic in various ways.

Activity 14.1

1 Open the publication called **COMPUTER**.

2 Change the screen display to **Fit in window**. This will make it easier when sizing the graphic.

3 CLICK on **File**.

4 CLICK on **Place**.

5 DOUBLE CLICK on your scanned file called **MODEL**.

6 Position the graphic pointer approximately in the middle of the text and CLICK.

Instructions

The scanned image should now appear on the publication but it may not be the size you require. The size of the graphic can be altered easily by putting handles on it, **pointing** at one of the handles in the corner, keeping the button down until a two-headed pointer appears and DRAGGING to the required size. When changing the size of a graphic take care that its shape does not become distorted. After changing the size you may wish to move it so it is centred on the text. Again you will need to put handles on the graphic, point roughly in the middle of it, keep the button down until a four-headed pointer appears and DRAG it to the new position. When you release the button the graphic will stop moving.

Activity 14.2

1 Select the **pointer tool** from the toolbox.

2 Put handles on your graphic by POINTING at it and CLICKING.

3 **Point** at the handles in one of the corners and DRAG until the correct size is achieved.

4 If necessary put handles on the graphic again.

5 POINT roughly in the middle of the graphic and DRAG it until it is centred on the text.

6 **Save** the publication calling it **COMPUTER**.

Key words

Placing a graphic
Sizing a graphic
Moving a graphic

Task 15 Changing the text wrap of a graphic to rectangular wrap

Objective To put a graphic boundary around the placed graphic, making the text wrap around it in a rectangular shape.

Instructions When you placed the graphic you did not ask for any particular type of text wrap, therefore the text flowed over the graphic making it difficult to read. You can opt for a particular text wrap before placing it. You are now going to change the way the text has wrapped around the graphic in the publication called **COMPUTER** and select the amount of space between the edge of the graphic and the text. This space can be altered at any time by selecting the **Text wrap** option again and changing the standoff measurements.

Activity 15.1

1 Open the publication called **COMPUTER**.

2 Select the **pointer tool** from the toolbox and CLICK on the graphic to put handles on it.

3 CLICK on **Options**.

4 CLICK on **Text wrap**.

A display similar to the following should be displayed.

Text wrap

O K

Cancel

Wrap options:

Text flow:

Standoff in mm

Left

Right

Top

Bottom

Instructions

The following options are available at the **Text wrap menu** and an explanation of these now follows.

No wrap option: the graphics boundary is deleted, therefore the text and graphics overwrite each other.

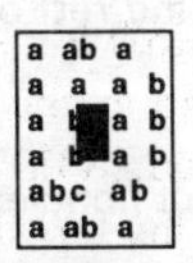

Rectangular wrap: a rectangular graphic boundary is created to the required measurments. The text will wrap around all sides of the graphic. This must be selected first before you can select the Text flow options.

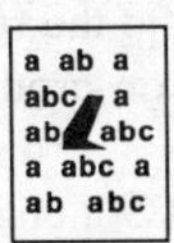

Custom wrap: this option is automatically selected by *PageMaker* when the graphic boundaries are manually adjusted.

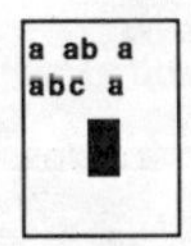

Column break: text will stop flowing at the top of the graphic and then jump to the top of the next column.

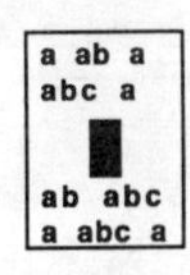

Jump over: text will jump over the graphic and continue flowing underneath.

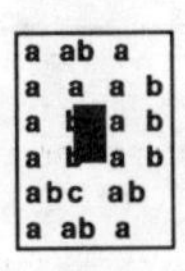

Wrap all sides: text will flow around all sides of the graphic.

Standoff: these are the boxes to enter the distance required between the graphic boundary and the graphic.

The current selections will appear in reverse.

Activity 15.2

1 CLICK on the **Rectangular wrap** icon.

2 CLICK on the **Wrap all sides** icon.

3 Enter **4mm** in each of the measurement boxes.

4 CLICK on **OK**.

The text should now have wrapped around the graphic. You will see a dotted line around the graphic which denotes the standoff area you entered in the measurement boxes.

Activity 15.3 The graphic may be too large to accommodate all the text on the page. You can still adjust its size. Note that when the graphic is selected as an object it still has the normal rectangular handles, but it also has diamond-shaped ones on the graphic boundary. Take care that you do not point at these when you are adjusting the size because they are used for custom wrap purposes. You will be using this in a later task. When you have changed the size look to see where the text is being wrapped around the graphic. It may be splitting a heading from the rest of the text. Move the graphic until it is in a more sensible position.

1 Using the **pointer tool** CLICK on the graphic to put handles on it.

2 POINT at and DRAG one of the rectangular handles to the required size of the graphic. When you release the button the text will wrap around to the new size.

3 POINT roughly at the middle of the graphic and DRAG it until you reach the required position for the graphic on the text.

4 **Save** your publication calling it **COMPUTER**.

Key words **Text wrap**
Rectangular wrap
Standoff area

Task 16 Changing the text wrap of a graphic to jump over

Objective

To put a graphic boundary around the placed graphic to make the text jump over it.

Instructions

Once a graphic has been placed the style of text wrap can be changed at any time. You are going to change the style from the previous task, rectangular wrap, to make the text jump over and continue underneath.

Activity

1 Open the publication called **COMPUTER**.

2 Select the **pointer tool** from the toolbox.

3 POINT at the graphic and CLICK to put handles on it.

4 CLICK on **Options**.

5 CLICK on **Text wrap**.

6 From the **Text flow options** CLICK on **Jump over**.

7 Change the top and bottom standoff measurements to **2.5 mm**.

8 If necessary change the size of the graphic so that all the text still fits on to the page.

9 Move the graphic so that all the text concerning the keyboard is situated after the graphic.

10 **Save** your publication calling it **COMPUTER**.

Key words **Jump over**

Task 17 **Changing the text wrap of a graphic to custom wrap**

Objective To change a graphic boundary to any irregular shape you require.

Instructions When you put handles on a graphic they appear in a rectangular shape and the text wrap options used so far only allow you to wrap around a graphic in a straight line. However, the boundary can be changed to any shape desired. This is done by DRAGGING the diamond-shaped handles to the required position. Extra diamond-shaped handles can be added by pointing at the required place on the dotted graphic boundary and CLICKING. To erase one of these handles DRAG it on top of another one. To prevent the publication continuously being re-drawn as you move the handles, hold down the SPACEBAR at the same time. When you release this the text will adjust to the new boundaries. You will need to select the **Rectangular wrap** option from the **Options menu** to ensure that the text wraps around the shape of the graphic.

Activity

1. Open the publication called **COMPUTER**.
2. Change the size of the screen display to **75%** to make it easier to distinguish between the rectangular and diamond-shaped handles.
3. Select the **pointer tool** from the toolbox.
4. POINT and CLICK to put handles on the graphic.
5. CLICK on **Options**.
6. CLICK on **Text wrap**.
7. CLICK on **Rectangular wrap**. There is no need to change any of the standoff measurements.
8. CLICK on **OK**.
9. If necessary, put extra handles on the boundary so that you can bring the boundary in, to wrap around the shape of the computer.
10. Hold down SPACEBAR, POINT at the diamond-shaped handles and DRAG them in towards the graphic to alter the shape of the boundary.

Key words **Custom wrap**
Diamond-shaped handles

Task 18 Adding and removing pages in a publication

Objective To insert and remove pages in an existing publication.

Instructions Pages can be added or removed at any time from a publication. You can have up to 128 pages in the publication, but it is better to work with smaller files than this because it can slow down the computer's response time. In this task you will practise displaying different pages on the screen.

Activity 18.1

1 CLICK on **File**.

2 CLICK on **New**.

3 Set up the page as **A4, tall, one page, not double-sided, margins** at **25 mm** each.

4 CLICK on **OK**.

5 CLICK on **Page**.

6 CLICK on **Insert pages . . .**

A display similar to the following should appear on the screen.

```
Insert pages                         ( O K )
                                     (Cancel)
Insert [1] page(s):

  ○ Before current page
  ◉ After current page
  ○ Between current pages
```

Instructions The following options are available at the **Insert pages menu** and these are now explained.

Before current page: this enables the insertion of the required number of pages before the one currently being worked.

After: this enables the insertion of the required number of pages after the one currently being worked.

Between current pages: this enables the insertion of pages between the current facing pages displayed on the screen.

Activity 18.2

1 CLICK on **Insert pages box** and enter **1**.

2 CLICK on **After current page** if it is not selected.

3 CLICK on **OK**.

Instructions

At the bottom of the screen you will see the page icons. At the moment page two is shown in reverse which indicates the page of the publication currently displayed on the screen. To display a different page you simply need to **point** at the page you wish to see and CLICK. Pages can be removed as easily as they are inserted. You can either remove just the page you have currently displayed or you can give instructions to remove a number of pages. However, you are prompted as to whether you wish to remove the pages and all of their contents. You are now going to remove the second page you have just inserted.

Activity 18.3

1 CLICK on **Page**.

2 CLICK on **Remove pages . . .**

A display similar to the following should appear on the screen.

```
Remove pages                    ( O K )
                                (Cancel)

Remove page(s)  [1]

       through  [1]
```

3 In the **Remove page** box enter **2**.

4 In the **through** box enter **2**.

5 CLICK on **OK**.

6 CLICK on **OK** again when prompted to remove the pages and their contents.

Key words	Adding pages Removing pages Displaying different pages

Task 19 Creating a dropped shadow

Objective

To layer boxes giving a three-dimensional effect.

Instructions

A dropped shadow effect is made up of a number of layered boxes which can be shaded to give a three-dimensional effect. Text can also be entered into the box in which case the top white box must be shaded with the paper shade. The **Send to back** and **Bring to front** options are used to change the order of the layers so that you can work on each one of them. In this task you are going to produce a box similar to the one below. To produce this you will need to draw a box and then copy it using the **Copy** option. The two copies of this box will then be pasted back on to the publication and the relevant shading will be applied. The boxes will be moved on top of each other, slightly offsetting each one, to give a dropped shadow effect with text placed in the top box. A dropped shadow can be achieved in a variety of ways with as many shadows as you wish.

TRAINING GUIDE

Activity

1 CLICK on **File**.

2 CLICK on **New**.

3 Set up the page as **A4 tall, one page, not double-sided, margins** at **25 mm** each.

4 CLICK on **OK**.

5 CLICK on **Page**.

6 CLICK on **75%** page display.

7 Select the **text tool** from the toolbox.

8 POINT and CLICK the **text pointer** on the page.

9 Type **TRAINING GUIDE** in any font, 16 point size and align to the centre.

10 CLICK on the **square corner tool** from the toolbox.

11 CLICK on **Lines**.

12 CLICK on **1pt**.

13 Position the **box pointer** on the page and draw a box around the text. There should not be any shading in this box at present.

14 With handles on the box CLICK on **Edit**.

15 CLICK on **Copy** to copy the box to the clipboard.

16 Select the **pointer tool** from the toolbox.

17 POINT and CLICK at your box surrounding the text to put handles on it.

18 CLICK on **Shades**.

19 CLICK on **Paper** to enable text to be written within this box.

20 With handles still on the box CLICK on **Edit**.

21 CLICK on **Send to back** as you need to send this box behind the text in order that the text can be seen.

22 CLICK on **Edit**.

23 CLICK on **Paste** to get a copy of the box currently on the clipboard.

24 With handles still on this copied box CLICK on **Shades**.

25 CLICK on **20%**.

26 POINT roughly at the middle of the shaded box and hold down the button until you get a four headed arrow icon.

27 DRAG the box over the top of the other one making it slightly offset.

28 With handles still on the shaded box CLICK on **Edit**.

29 CLICK on **Send to back**.

30 CLICK on **Edit**.

31 CLICK on **Paste**.

32 With handles still on the copied box CLICK on **Shades**.

33 CLICK on **Solid**.

34 POINT roughly at the middle of the solid box and hold down the button until you get a four headed arrow icon.

35 DRAG the box over the top of the other ones making it slightly offset.

36 With handles still on the shaded box CLICK on **Edit**.

37 CLICK on **Send to back**.

You should now have three boxes layered with text inside the top box.

Key words **Copy**
Shades
Send to back
Dropped shadows

Task 20

Creating reverse text

Objective

To enter text which will appear as white text on a black background.

Instructions

You are going to enter text which will appear as the opposite to normal, i.e. usually text is black on a white background but when reversed it will appear as white text on a black background. One way of achieving this is to enter the text, draw a box round it which will be shaded as a solid later, and change the text to reverse. Take care because reverse text, without a solid background around it, is difficult to see because it becomes white text on a white background. The reverse text can enhance the final output of the publication. It is also useful if you are producing work with instructions as these could be highlighted.

Also during this task you will see that you can select the type font, size and alignment before keying in the text.

Activity

1 CLICK on **File**.

2 CLICK on **New** and set up the following page specifications:
A4, tall, one page, not double-sided, margins 25 mm each.

3 CLICK on **Page**.

4 CLICK on **75%** page size.

5 Select the **text tool** from the toolbox.

6 POINT and CLICK the text pointer on the page.

7 CLICK on **Type**.

8 CLICK on **Type specs**.

9 CLICK on **Helv 16** point.

10 CLICK on **OK**.

11 CLICK on **Type**.

12 CLICK on **Align** centre.

13 Key in **Wendy Chuter**.

14 Select the **square corner box** from the toolbox.

15 Select **Shades**.

16 Select **None**.

17 Draw a box around the text.

18 Select the **text tool** from the toolbox.

19 TRIPLE CLICK on the **text** to highlight it.

20 CLICK on **Type**.

21 CLICK on **Reverse**.

22 Select the **pointer tool** from the toolbox.

23 CLICK on the **box** to put handles on it.

24 CLICK on **Shades**.

25 CLICK on **Solid**.

26 With handles still on the box, CLICK on **Edit**.

27 CLICK on **Send to back**.

Key words	**Reverse**

Task 21 Creating columns

Objective

To work with columns on the page, setting the margins between the columns, customising their position on the page and locking them into place.

Instructions

You are going to set up a page which will have three columns on it similar to the one below.

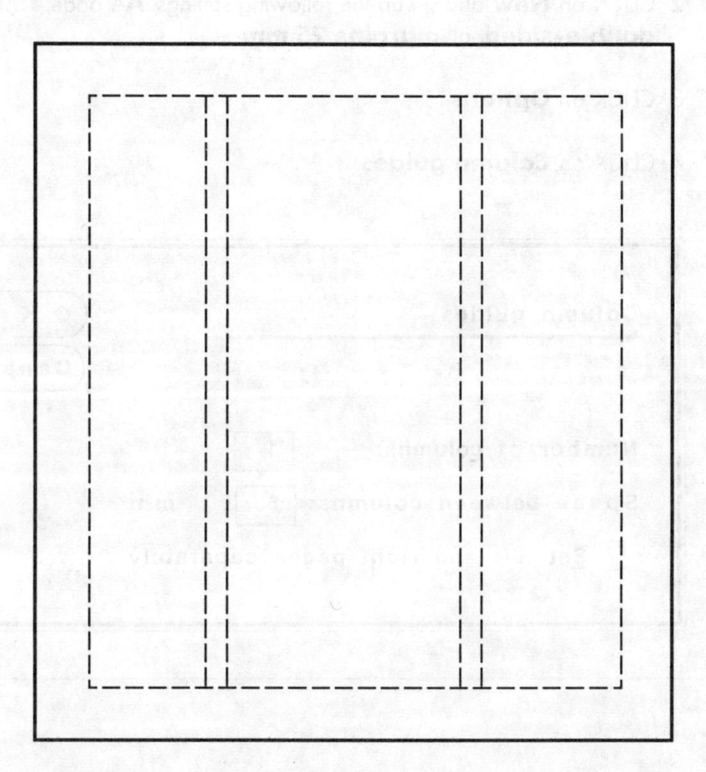

When columns are set up *PageMaker* takes the number of columns requested, the amount of space requested between each column, and divides the page into equal columns between the current margins. Up to twenty columns can be used and all the columns on the page must have the same amount of space between them. When unequal columns are required the column is dragged to the required position. It is a good idea to lock the columns into position to safeguard against accidentally moving them. When columns are set, any text already on the page will not automatically reformat to the size of the column width. Only new text entered or placed text will be affected. The **Column guide** option can also help to divide the page up into equal parts by changing the space between the columns to zero. Guidelines can be placed on top of the column markers. By going back to the **Column guides** option the number of required columns can be set and DRAGGED to the position of the guidelines.

Activity 21.1 Set up a one page publication and use the **Column guides** option to divide the page into four equal parts. Then draw guidelines on top of these column guides to assist with the customising of a three column layout.

1 CLICK on **File**.

2 CLICK on **New** and set up the following settings, **A4** page, **tall** size, **not double-sided**, all **margins 25 mm**.

3 CLICK on **Options**.

4 CLICK on **Column guides**.

Column guides	
	O K
	Cancel
Number of columns:	1
Space between columns:	5 mm
☐ Set left and right pages separately	

Instructions The following options are available at the **Column guides menu** and these are now explained.

Number of columns: this enables the stipulation of the number of columns required on the page.

Space between columns: this enables the stipulation of the amount of space required between the columns.

Set left and right pages separately: this enables the setting of a different number of columns on left- and right-hand pages. This is only available when the **Facing pages** option is selected on the **Page setup** menu.

Activity 21.2

1 Divide the page into four equal parts by keying in **4** in the number of columns and entering a **zero** in the space between the columns.

2 CLICK on **OK**.

3 POINT at the vertical ruler and DRAG a guideline across and place it on top of the first column guide (i.e. the second vertical line in from the left).

4 POINT at the vertical ruler and DRAG a second guideline across and place it on top of the third column (i.e. the second vertical line from the right).

Activity 21.3

Now change the number of columns to **three** with **5 mm** space between them. The middle column guides will then be DRAGGED across to the guidelines just set. This will give the same display as the one on p. 47. Finally the columns will be locked into position to prevent you accidentally moving them.

1 CLICK on **Options**.

2 CLICK on **Column guides**.

3 Enter **3** in the **Number of columns** box.

4 Enter **5** in the **Space between columns** box.

5 CLICK on **OK**.

6 CLICK on **Options** and deselect **Snap to** guides, **Snap to** rulers and **Lock** guides (a tick alongside the options means they are selected) to turn off the magnetic pull. This will allow you to DRAG the columns so that the guidelines are situated in the middle of the column space.

7 CLICK on **Page** and select **75%** size to make it easier to see the positioning of the column guides in relation to the guidelines.

8 POINT at the space between the first column guide, hold down the button until a two headed arrow icon appears, DRAG the column towards the left until the vertical guideline is in the middle of the space between the column, then release.

9 POINT at the space between the second column guide, hold down the button until a two headed arrow icon appears, DRAG the column to the right until the vertical guideline is in the middle of the space between the column, then release.

10 CLICK on **Options**.

11 CLICK on **Lock guides**.

You should now have the required page layout.

Key words **Column guides**
Customise columns
Lock guides

Task 22 Creating a master page

Objective

To create a master page with three columns, a header and automatic page numbering.

Instructions

A master page is created when common items such as headers, footers, text, graphics, guides, columns and automatic page numbering are required on every page throughout the publication. When objects are entered on to a numbered page they will only appear on that page. Once an object has been entered on to a master page no alteration can be made to it, unless you go to the master page. It is quicker to set up a master page for the common elements which are going to appear throughout the publication. A single-sided publication has only one master page while a double-sided one has two. You are now going to start a new publication and set a header on the master page. This header will then appear in the same place on every page throughout the publication.

Activity 22.1

The header that you are to set up should appear at the top right on the master page.

1 CLICK on **File**.

2 CLICK on **New** and set up the following page specifications:
A4, tall, 2 pages, not double-sided, margins 25 mm each.

3 CLICK on **OK**.

4 CLICK on the **R** in the bottom left corner of the screen for the master icon page.

5 Select the **text tool** from the toolbox.

6 CLICK the **text pointer** at the top of the page.

7 Key in **PORTSMOUTH HOTELS**

8 TREBLE CLICK on the word **PORTSMOUTH** to highlight the line.

9 CLICK on **Type**.

10 CLICK on **Type specs**.

11 Select **Helv 12 point** (or any other font and size available).

12 CLICK on **OK**.

13 While the word is still highlighted CLICK on **Type**.

14 CLICK on **Align right**.

15 Select the **pointer tool** from the toolbox.

16 POINT and CLICK at the text to put handles on it.

17 POINT and hold down the button until a four arrowed icon appears.

18 DRAG the text until it is positioned above the top margin guide and release.

Activity 22.2 Now set up the automatic page numbering feature and place it as a footer, aligned to the centre. To enter the automatic page feature hold down CTRL and SHIFT keys together and type **3**. The automatic page number on a master page will appear as a 0 but the correct numbers will appear on the individual pages. If the page number is required in brackets, with a dash either side or the word *Page* to precede it, then enter the required characters before pressing the automatic page feature.

1 Select the **text tool** from the tool box.

2 CLICK on **text pointer** at the bottom of the page.

3 Hold down the CTRL and SHIFT keys together and enter **3**.

4 DOUBLE CLICK on the **0** to highlight it.

5 CLICK on **Type**.

6 CLICK on **Type specs**.

7 Select **Helv 12** point (or any font and size available).

8 CLICK on **OK**.

9 While the page number is still highlighted CLICK on **Type**.

10 CLICK on **Align centre**.

11 Select the **pointer tool** from the toolbox.

12 POINT and CLICK at the page number to put handles on it.

13 POINT and hold down the button until a four-arrowed icon appears.

14 DRAG the text until it is positioned just below the bottom margin and release.

Activity 22.4

You are now going to set the publication up with three columns.

1 CLICK on **Options**.

2 CLICK on **Column guides**.

3 Key in **3** in the **Number of columns**.

4 Key in **6 mm** in the **Space between columns**.

5 CLICK on **OK**.

6 CLICK on **Options**.

7 CLICK on **Lock guides** to select the option (if a tick already appears alongside, then it has been selected).

8 **Save** this publication for future use calling it **HOTEL**.

Activity 22.5

You have now set up the master page containing the header, the page number and three columns which will appear on every page throughout the publication. You can check this by CLICKING on the page icons.
You will see that each page contains the header and columns and that the relevant page numbers appear at the bottom.
Before entering the text into the publication you must remember to display the relevant page, otherwise you will still be working on the master page.

Key words

Master page
Header
Automatic page number

Task 23 Creating styles

Objective

To define different styles which will enable the alteration of fonts, pitch and alignment of selected text quickly.

Instructions

You are going to define different styles and apply them to different parts of the text. This command is very useful and can save time. When word processed text is imported it will normally be in exactly the same font and pitch size throughout. By defining styles and highlighting selected text the required style can be applied to it. You may find that there are already defined styles in PageMaker. The different styles are selected by displaying the **Style palette** and selecting the required style. The defined styles are saved with the publication. It is also possible to copy a style from one publication to another, thereby saving you from having to define the styles on every publication. You are going to edit and set up four different styles on the master page created in the previous task. Remember during this task that a cross or a filled-in circle means that the option has been selected.

Activity 23.1

Edit the body text to have the following style: **Helv 12** size, **Automatic hyphenation, Alignment left, First indent 6 mm**.

1 CLICK on **File**.

2 CLICK on **Open**.

3 Open your publication called **HOTEL**.

4 CLICK on **Type**.

5 CLICK on **Define styles**. A display similar to the following should appear on the screen.

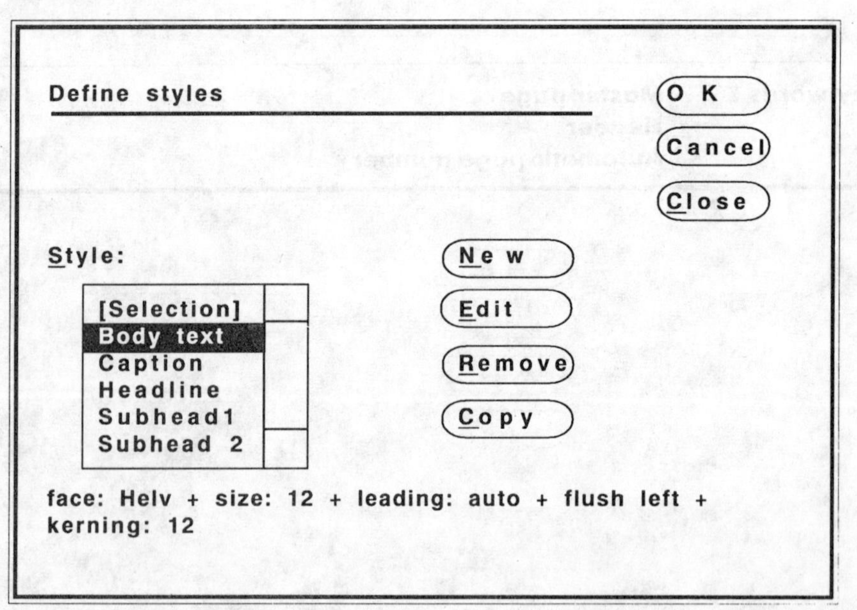

Instructions

The following options are available at the **Define styles menu** and an explanation of these now follows:

New: this enables a new style to be defined.

Edit: this enables an existing style to be changed.

Remove: this enables an existing style to be erased.

Copy: this enables a style to be copied from one publication to another.

Activity 23.2

1 CLICK on **Body text**.

2 CLICK on **Edit**. A display similar to the following should appear on the screen.

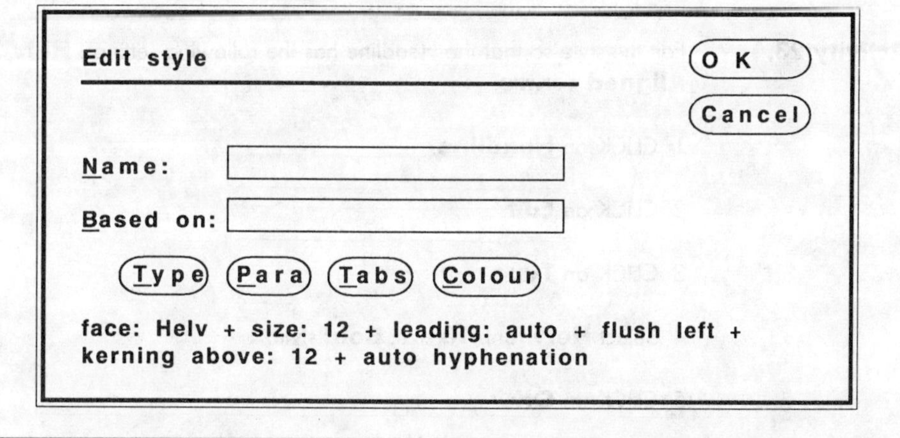

Instructions

The following options are available at the **Edit menu** of **Defining styles** and an explanation of these now follows:

Name: this enables the style to be given a name or to display the current style name.

Based on: this enables a new style to be based on an old one by editing it.

Type: this option displays the **Type specifications menu** where the font, pitch size, any underlining, bold etc, can be selected.

Para: this option displays the **Paragraph specifications menu** where automatic hyphenation, the alignment of the text, and the measurements of any indents can be set.

Tabs: this option allows tab settings to be set.

Colours: this option enables colours for the publication to be selected, but you will require a colour printer to print out in colour.

Activity 23.3

1 CLICK on **Type**.

2 Select **Helv** font, **12** size and **Normal** style.

3 CLICK on **OK**.

4 CLICK on **Para**.

5 Select **Auto hyphenation, Alignment left**, and enter **6 mm** in the **First indents** box.

6 CLICK on **OK**.

7 CLICK on **OK**.

Activity 23.4

Edit the style so that the Headline has the following settings: **Helv 18** size, **Bold, Aligned centre**.

1 CLICK on **Headline**.

2 CLICK on **Edit**.

3 CLICK on **Type**.

4 Select **Helv** font, **18** size, **Bold** style.

5 CLICK on **OK**.

6 CLICK on **Para**.

7 Select **No automatic hyphenation, Alignment centre, 0** in all the **Indents** boxes.

8 CLICK on **OK**.

9 CLICK on **OK**.

Activity 23.5

Now edit the style for Subhead 1 to have the following settings: **Helv 14** size, **Underline, no left indent**.

1 CLICK on **Subhead 1**.

2 CLICK on **Edit**.

3 CLICK on **Type**.

4 Select **Helv** font, **14** size, **Underline** style.

5 CLICK on **OK**.

6 CLICK on **Para**.

7 Select **No hyphenation, Alignment left, 0** in all the **indents** boxes.

8 CLICK on **OK**.

9 CLICK on **OK**.

Activity 23.6

Now create a new style based on the body text, where the font and pitch size will be the same, but there will be no automatic hyphenation selected and the left and right indents will be set at **3 mm** with no first line indent.

1 CLICK on **New**.

2 Enter **LIST** in the **Name box** and delete **Subhead 1** from the **Based on box**.

3 CLICK on **Type**.

4 Select **Helv** font, **12** size, **Normal** style.

5 CLICK on **OK**.

6 CLICK on **Para**.

7 Select **no automatic hyphenation, Alignment justify**, enter **3 mm** in both Left and Right **Indent** boxes, and **0** in the **First indent** box.

8 CLICK on **OK**.

9 CLICK on **OK**. Note that this style has now been added to the names of the styles which can be selected.

10 CLICK on **OK** to finish defining styles.

Activity 23.7 You will need to display the style palette on the screen in order to use the various styles.

1 CLICK on **Options**.

2 CLICK on **Style palette**.

3 **Save** the publication calling it **HOTEL**.

Key words

Defining styles
Displaying the style palette

Task 24 **Using the styles palette**

Objective To use the styles palette and apply it to selected text.

Instructions In the previous task you defined styles of text. You are now going to apply these styles to the text in your publication. By selecting the required block of text and the required style, the font, size and alignment of the text can be easily changed. You can use the style palette for any text imported from a word processor or you can select the style and then key in the text. If, after using the Style palette you edit a style, it will automatically change any text using the style currently.

Activity 24.1 Before starting this task you will need to enter the following text, preferably on to a word processor, ready for it to be placed into the publication. **Save** the file calling it **PORTS**. However, it can be entered directly into the publication, when only one font, one size and left alignment should be used. You will open the publication you created with styles in Task 23 and apply the styles to the relevant text.

The maritime traditions of the City of Portsmouth can be traced back as far as 1194 when King Richard I ordered the construction of the first naval dock. Today, the dockyard is home to the following:

Mary Rose with her fascinating Tudor artefacts

Nelson's HMS Victory

HMS Warrior, which was the first 'iron clad' warship

The New Hotel, Portsmouth stands at the entrance of the harbour. It is a short distance from the City Centre and the nearby motorways. There is easy access to the surrounding countryside, and for the ferries to the Continent, the Channel Islands and the Isle of Wight.

The facilities at The New Hotel are impressive. The Harbour Restaurant offers excellent à la carte dishes, which you can watch being prepared in the exhibition kitchen. For a less formal meal, the snack menu is available from early till late.

Our guest rooms are really spacious: most contain two double beds and all feature individual temperature control, colour television with 'in-room' videos and, of course, a private bathroom.

But perhaps the most exciting feature of The New Hotel is the fitness facility. Here, together under one roof you will find the heated swimming pool, warm-water whirlpool, exercise equipment, sauna solarium and even two squash courts. What better way to ease away the tensions of a busy day?

Conference and Banquet Facilities

As you will see The New Hotel is an ideal location for your next conference or banquet. Our experienced management and staff look forward to welcoming you. All the conference and meeting rooms at the hotel have been carefully designed to give you the maximum choice of style and layout and are air-conditioned for extra comfort. Conferences for up to 300 delegates can be accommodated in the Mary Rose Suite, up to 150 in the Nelson Suite and there are seven stylish meeting rooms, each accommodating 16 delegates. The Warrior Suite divides into two and can accommodate either 20 or 30 delegates, or when combined, it will hold 50 in comfort. Should 'new model' vehicles or displays form part of your conference, cars or light vans can be driven directly into the Mary Rose Suite.

The New Hotel 'presenter pack' provides the conference organiser with a comprehensive range of audio-visual and presentation equipment. All the equipment is readily available for hire at the hotel at very competitive prices and eliminates the problem of transport. A detailed list of the equipment available, together with full details on the function suites and rooms are available on request.

The skill and expertise of the management and staff at The New Hotel, Portsmouth will make the planning of your banquet so much easier.

Our Banqueting Manager can take a lot of the weight off your shoulders by helping you with such matters as printing the invitations, arranging the supply of flowers, the hiring of guest speakers, bar arrangements and the selection of a menu to suit both your taste and budget.

Here at The New Hotel we have a great deal of experience in catering for all types of banquets, from intimate family gatherings to large scale formal functions and we have the right rooms to suit all types. At the higher end of the scale, the Mary Rose Suite can accommodate up to 28 guests at a banquet or 250 for a dinner-dance. The Nelson Suite can cater for 130 and 100 respectively and the Warrior Suite can seat 50 at a banquet. Full details of room sizes and layouts are available. Guests attending the functions can stay overnight at a special rate and those with children will be especially pleased to know that children sharing their parents' room are accommodated free of charge.

Activity 24.2 Now place the word processed text and select from the different styles created in the previous task and apply them to the text. You will see that the imported text flows on to two pages and that all the text on these pages can be changed with one instruction.

1 CLICK on **File**.

2 CLICK on **Open**.

3 Select the publication called **HOTEL** and ensure that page one is displayed on the screen.

4 CLICK on **Options**.

5 CLICK on **Autoflow** to select it (a tick alongside denotes it has already been selected).

6 CLICK on **File**.

7 CLICK on **Place**.

8 DOUBLE CLICK on the word processed file **PORTS**.

9 Position the autoflow pointer at the top of the first column and CLICK.

10 Select the **text tool** from the toolbox.

11 CLICK anywhere in the text.

12 CLICK on **Edit**.

13 CLICK on **Select all** (this will select all the text on both pages of the publication).

14 If the **Style palette** is not displayed CLICK on **Options** and CLICK on **Style palette**.

15 To change all the imported text, CLICK on **Body text** in the **Styles palette**.

16 CLICK on **Page one icon**.

17 Position and CLICK the text pointer before the **M** of 'Mary Rose with her . . .'.

18 DRAG down to highlight as far as ' . . . iron-clad warship'.

19 CLICK on **List** in the Style palette.

20 **Scroll** the page to find the paragraph heading 'Hotel Facilities', probably in the first column.

21 TREBLE CLICK to highlight.

22 CLICK on **Subhead 1** in the **Style palette**.

23 TREBLE CLICK on the paragraph heading 'Conference and Banquet Facilities'.

24 CLICK on **Subhead 1** in the **Style palette**.

25 CLICK on **File**.

26 **Save** the publication calling it **HOTEL**.

Key words	Using defined styles Autoflow

Task 25

Changing the length of the text blocks in columns

Objective

To adjust the length of text blocks by using the handles attached to them.

Instructions

When text is imported into a publication it flows to the bottom of the columns. However, when you look at the text you may find that a heading has been split from its paragraph, or you wish to leave a space for a future graphic or headline. This task will instruct you how to leave a gap at the top of the publication for a future headline and a space at the bottom of the first page for a future graphic. Guidelines will be used to help you to achieve this. Column lengths are adjusted by putting handles on the relevant column and dragging the character in the loop either up or down, depending upon whether you wish to increase or decrease the column length. Ensure the mouse button is kept depressed otherwise you will pick up the rest of the text.

Activity 25.1

Open the publication called **HOTEL** and set two guidelines on the first page at **40 mm** and **230 mm**. These guidelines will assist you to ensure all the columns start and end at exactly the same place.

1 CLICK on **File.**

2 CLICK on **Open**.

3 **Open** the publication called HOTEL.

4 If Page 1 is not displayed CLICK on the **icon** for **page 1**. Display at **Fit in window** size.

5 POINT at the horizontal ruler and DRAG a guideline down to **40 mm**.

6 DRAG another guideline down to **230 mm**.

7 Select the **pointer tool** from the toolbox.

8 POINT and CLICK at the first column to put handles on it.

9 POINT at the top empty loop, hold down the button and DRAG down to the guideline at **40 mm**, then release the button.

10 POINT at the + in the bottom loop, hold down the button and DRAG up to the guideline at **230 mm**, then release the button.

11 Repeat steps 8–10 for the other columns on page 1.

12 CLICK on **Page 2 icon**.

13 The second column on page 2 may not have flowed into the third column, as you altered the pitch size after it had flowed in.

14 CLICK on the **second column** to put handles on it.

15 POINT at the + in the bottom loop, hold down and DRAG it up to the bottom margin, then release the button.

16 CLICK on the + in the bottom loop to pick up the text.

17 Position the autoflow pointer at the top of the third column and CLICK.

18 If you wish you can read through the publication and adjust the endings of the columns if some of them do not end in a sensible position.

19 **Save** the publication calling it **HOTEL**.

Key words **Text column lengths**

Task 26 Spreading a headline across several columns

Objective

To enter a headline into a column and spread it across several columns

Instructions

In the previous task you left a large gap at the top of the first page to accommodate a headline. When columns are set up any text you key in will automatically have the block width of that column. Sometimes you may wish to have a headline which will span more than one column. To do this, first put handles on the text keyed in and DRAG the width of the block of text to the required measurement. You can then enter a headline for the publication from the previous task and centre it across the three columns. You will also see that you can select a style before keying in text.

Activity 26.1

1 CLICK on **File**.

2 CLICK on **Open**.

3 **Open** the publication called **HOTEL**.

4 Ensure that you have page 1 displayed on the screen and the **style palette** is displayed.

5 Select the **text tool** from the toolbox.

6 Select **Headline** from the **Style palette**.

7 CLICK the **text pointer** in the space above the **4 mm** guideline.

8 Type **THE NEW HOTEL PORTSMOUTH**.

9 Select the **pointer tool** from the toolbox.

10 POINT and CLICK at **THE NEW HOTEL PORTSMOUTH** to put handles on it.

11 POINT at one of the right handles, hold down until a two-headed icon appears, DRAG across until the block width meets the right margin, then release the button.

12 CLICK on **Options** and deselect **Snap to guides** if it is currently selected. This will help you with the next step.

13 If the text is not centred vertically in the top space, then while you still have handles on the text, POINT to the middle of the block, hold down until a four-headed icon appears, DRAG the text down until it is in the middle of the space at the top and release the button.

Key words **Speading a headline**

Task 27 Typing special characters

Objective

To type special characters – the bullet, the registered trademark and the copyright sign.

Instructions

While keying in your publication you may wish to enter some special characters which do not appear on the keyboard. These characters can be entered by using a combination of keystrokes.

Activity

Set up a new page and practise entering these special characters. The bullet character looks like a filled-in circle or large, raised full stop; the copyright sign appears as a letter C within a circle; and the registered trademark is a letter R within a circle. Their sizes can be changed in the same way as any other character.

1 To type the bullet, select the text tool from the toolbox and CLICK the icon at the required position in your publication

Hold down SHIFT and CTRL together and press **8**

2 To type a copyright sign, hold down SHIFT and CTRL together and type a letter **C**

3 To type the registered trademark sign, hold down SHIFT and CTRL together and type a letter **R**

Key words

Typing a bullet
Typing a copyright sign
Typing a registered trademark

Task 28 **Consolidation exercise**

Objective To consolidate learning of the topics covered in this *Guide.*

Instructions Throughout this book you have been introduced to a variety of topics. This task aims to test your knowledge of how to:

set up a new page
use a master page to set up columns
use a header and a footer
set up styles to be applied later to imported text
place a graphic and draw a box around it
spread a headline across two columns
change the headline to reverse text

Activity 28.1 Set up a new publication according to the following specifications:

A4, tall, 1 page, not double-sided, margins 30 mm each.

Set up a master page with two columns with 5 mm between the columns.

Set up three styles ot text:

1 Body Text to be 10 points, a type style of your choice, justified text with no indentation.

2 Headline to be 24 points, a type style of your choice, with text aligned to the centre.

3 Sub-head to be 12 points, a type style of your choice, with text aligned to the left.

Set up the following header and footer:

Key in today's date as the header in Body Text style.

Number the page as a footer in Body Text style.

Activity 28.2 The following text needs to be entered into a word processor and placed into the publication using the Autoflow facility.

THE EUROPEAN COMMUNITY

What is it?

The European Community is a unique grouping of 12 sovereign European member states committed to the development of closer economic and political cooperation.

The Community has agreed to break down the economic and political barriers that have traditionally divided Europe. In particular, it seeks to encourage greater freedom of movement, not only of goods but also of services, capital and people between its member states.

Why?

For centuries, war plagued the Continent of Europe. On two occasions this century, European quarrels spilled over into world conflicts in which more than 40 million people died.

The European Community is a bold attempt to prevent that from happening again. By encouraging the sharing of national sovereignty, the harmful effects of unchecked nationalism can be curbed.

In today's world, problems of unemployment, economic growth or the global environment can no longer be tackled by national governments acting alone. The costs, for example, of undertaking innovative research programmes or of developing new competitive technologies are now such that it makes sense for European countries to work together more closely for the common good. This will ensure that the European Community's members can continue to have a collective influence in the world equal to their economic importance and history.

The Institutions

The major decision-making body of the European Community is the Council of Ministers. The Council is composed of Government Ministers from each member state. Since the Single European Act of 1987, many more decisions are taken by majority rather than unanimous vote. However, the United Kingdom, like any nation, can veto a proposal vitally affecting its national interest.

The Council acts mainly on proposals from the European Commission, the policy-planning body of the Community, whose 17 nationally-appointed members are under oath to act independently in the interests of the Community as a whole.

Before the Council can take a final decision, proposed legislation has to be scrutinised by the 518 members of the European Parliament. Britain, France, Germany and Italy all have 81 directly elected MEPs. Smaller member states have seats broadly in accordance with their populations.

The Economic and Social Committee is also formally consulted on policy and legislation. The Committee represents the interests of industry, trade unions and other Community-wide social and economic groups, including the consumer.

Activity 28.3 Apply the three different styles created in Activity 28.1 to the imported text in 28.2.

The Headline needs to be cut from the text, pasted back, spreading it across the two columns, and then altered to reverse text.

Activity 28.4 You will need to scan the image below or select an image supplied with the program.

This image needs to be placed at the bottom of the second column. You may need to adjust its size and then draw a 2 pt square box around the graphic. Adjust the column endings if necessary, to ensure that they are split in a sensible place.

Save your publication.

Key word	**Consolidation**

Task 29

Consolidation exercise

Objective

To consolidate learning of the topics covered in this *Guide.*

Instructions

This task aims to test your knowledge of how to open a publication, change the position and graphic boundary of a graphic, redefine styles, and create a dropped shadow.

Activity

Open the publication you saved in Task 28.

Move the graphic from the bottom of the second column to the middle of the page.

Customise the graphic boundary so the text wraps around the graphic in an irregular shape.

Change the style for the Sub-head to 14 points, italic and underline.

Remove the reverse text from the Headline and create a dropped shadow effect in its place.

Key word **Consolidation**